Call to Action: An Intentional Journey to break unhealthy patterns in our marriage Covenant

Workbook

By

Boatemaa

Copyright © 2025 by – Boatemaa – All Rights Reserved.

No part of this book may be reproduced or transmitted in any form by any means, whether graphic, electronic, or mechanical, including photography, recording, taping, or by any information storage or retrieval system, without prior written permission from the author.

Dedication

I dedicate this book to my parents, whose influence and example have shaped my understanding of love, respect, and partnership. Growing up in a home where my father cooked and cleaned, and my mother ran her own salon, I witnessed firsthand the power of mutual respect and support. Despite any disagreements they might have had, they always communicated with care and showed concern for one another, teaching me what true partnership looks like. Even after an argument, their love and support for each other remained unwavering.

My parents have been the bedrock of my marriage from the very beginning, and I am forever grateful for the foundation they have laid.

Mom, I truly miss you.

Acknowledgments

First and foremost, I want to give all glory to my Father in Heaven, God, the Alpha and Omega of my life, whose love, grace, and power are the foundation of every word in this book. Without His guidance, strength, and wisdom, this work would not be possible. I am humbled by His constant presence, wisdom, anointing, and provision in my life and in my marriage.

To my beloved husband, Fred, thank you for being my partner, the one who walks beside me through both the highs and the lows. Your unwavering love and commitment to our marriage give me the courage to take this leap of faith, and the example you set for our family and our community inspires me daily.

To my children, Joshua and Isabell, thank you for your love, understanding, and support as I've poured my heart into this book.

Your presence has helped shape the woman I am today, and I am forever grateful to you both.

I am also deeply grateful to the couples and families I've had the privilege of walking alongside. Your stories, struggles, and triumphs have taught me more about the power of faith, forgiveness, and resilience than I could ever express. This book is as much your testimony as it is mine.

To those who have supported me spiritually through prayer, whether near or far, thank you for your prayers and encouragement.

Lastly, to anyone reading these words, thank you for taking the time to invest in your marriage and your relationship with God. I pray that you find hope, restoration, and renewed love as you journey through the pages of this book.

It is my deepest prayer that God will use this work to bring healing and transformation into your life.

With heartfelt gratitude,

Boatemaa

About the Author

Boatemaa holds a degree in Mental Health Social Work and is a devoted advocate for marriage and family restoration. With over 26 years of marriage to her husband Fred, a retired military veteran, Boatemaa brings both professional insight and personal experience to her ministry.

Together, they are the proud parents of two children, Joshua and Isabell.

Boatemaa writes from a place of authenticity and faith, blending biblical truth with compassionate wisdom. Her passion is to help couples rebuild their connection through God's love, encouraging intentional care, open communication, and spiritual intimacy. Through her writing, speaking, and mentoring, Boatemaa offers hope and practical guidance for couples in every season of marriage.

Alongside her husband, she teaches marriage workshops and couples' classes, equipping others with tools to strengthen their relationship and deepen their walk with God. Whether writing, mentoring, or speaking,

Boatemaa's mission remains the same: to remind couples that no marriage is beyond healing—and that with God at the center, any relationship can be renewed.

When she's not writing or teaching, Boatemaa enjoys spending quality time with her family, pouring into others, and watching marriages transform through the power of grace and truth.

Table of Contents

Dedication...ii

Acknowledgments iii

About the Author..v

Introduction..1

Chapter 1 Marriage: A Reflection on Love, Honor, and Covenant..4

Chapter 2 Our Idea of Marriage vs. God's Idea of Marriage.............7

Chapter 3 Renewing Our Commitment to God Renews Our Marriage...10

Chapter 4 Committing Through the Struggles.................................13

Chapter 5 Built for Connection, Bound by Conviction....................17

Chapter 6 Restoring Your Marriage: Let Go of the Past and Choose Love...20

Chapter 7 Staying in Love 28

Chapter 8 Building a Strong, Firm Foundation in Your Marriage..33

Chapter 9 Avoiding an Empty Marriage...42

Introduction

Welcome to this workbook on building a strong, faith-filled marriage.

When writing this book, my heart was to speak directly to the real struggles, patterns, and behaviors that can quietly erode the foundation of a marriage, by addressing what *love* truly means, not according to the world's definition, but in the context of God's truth.

We all bring habits, wounds, and reactions into our relationships that, if left unchecked, can create distance and damage. But through the power of the Holy Spirit, we can recognize these patterns, break free from them, and begin to restore what has been lost.

This workbook is designed to help you reflect on your commitment, not just to your spouse, but to the sacred covenant you made before God. Each chapter invites you to deepen your connection with God and your partner, examine your heart, and realign your marriage with God's vision.

Whether your relationship is in a season of struggle or simply in need of a fresh spark of intentionality, this journey is for you. As you engage with the readings, scriptures, journaling prompts, and prayer, my hope is that you will keep an open heart, a willingness to listen to the Holy Spirit, and choose humility over pride—so you can grow closer to each other and to the One who created marriage in the first place.

With God at the center, no marriage is beyond hope.

Let's begin.

—Boatemaa

How to Use This Workbook

A Guide for Couples, Classes, and Small Groups

This workbook is designed to guide you and your spouse through a journey of reflection, healing, and reconnection—anchored in God's truth and grace. Whether you're using it on your own, as a couple, or in a class setting, follow these steps for a meaningful experience:

1. Read Slowly and Prayerfully

Take your time with each chapter. Read with intention and humility, and allow the Holy Spirit to guide you. Begin each session with prayer, asking God to soften your heart and reveal truth.

2. Journal Your Responses

Engage fully with the reflection questions and journaling prompts. Write honestly. These responses are for your spiritual and emotional growth—don't rush through them. This process works best when you invite God into your self-reflection.

3. Complete the Questionnaire (Before and After)

At the back of this workbook is a detailed marriage questionnaire.

- **Step 1:** Each spouse should complete the questionnaire **individually** before starting the workbook.

- **Step 2:** After finishing the entire workbook, revisit the questionnaire **together** as a couple. Discuss how your answers and perspectives may have changed and where you've seen growth.

Group/Class Tip: The questionnaire can be used as a powerful tool for group discussions. It fosters vulnerability, encourages shared wisdom, and builds real connection.

4. Use in a Class or Small Group

If you're using this workbook in a class setting, consider working through the reflection questions and activities together. Use the **questionnaire** as a foundation for open, honest discussions. It's a great way to deepen community and support one another in the journey of marriage.

5. End Each Chapter with a Prayer

Conclude every session by praying alone or together. Invite God to help you apply what you've learned and to bless your efforts to grow in love, humility, and unity.

6. Extend Grace

This is a journey—not a checklist. You and your spouse are learning and growing together. Be patient. Be kind. Celebrate progress, and don't expect perfection. Where there is humility, love, and God's presence, there is always hope.

With God at the center, your marriage can be renewed, restored, and stronger than ever.

Chapter 1
Marriage: A Reflection on Love, Honor, and Covenant

Here's a truth we don't hear often enough: **our marriage is not just about us.**

From the very beginning, marriage was part of God's divine plan. When God said, *"Let us make man in our image,"* both male and female were in His heart. That moment reveals something deeply intentional—**man and woman were not afterthoughts**, and neither was marriage. It was designed with purpose, order, and holiness. Marriage today often loses sight of that design. We enter it with hopes of personal fulfillment, but God calls us to something deeper. In marriage, we're meant to **understand one another**, to care deeply about each other's joys, struggles, needs, and dreams. That kind of unity requires **a love rooted in Christ**, a willingness to **humble ourselves**, and a daily commitment to **die to selfishness**. If you're married and feel that disconnect, don't ignore it. Don't settle for surviving. **Seek help. Invite God in.** Surround yourselves with wise counsel, prayer, and community. Healing and restoration are possible because God's design for marriage hasn't changed.

Reflection Questions:

1. What were your initial expectations of marriage? How did you imagine it would be?

   _____
   _____
   _____

2. How do you currently define "honor" in your marriage? What does it look like day-to-day?

3. Reflect on a moment in your marriage where you felt true love and commitment. What made that moment special?

4. Think about a challenge you have faced in your marriage. How did your commitment to one another help you get through it?

Activity: The Dream Marriage vs. Reality

- **Step 1:** Write a list of what your "dream marriage" looks like—based on TV shows, movies, or societal expectations.

- **Step 2:** Now, make a list of the realities of your marriage—what are the challenges? What are the joys?

- **Step 3:** How can you bring the two together? What steps can you take to align your marriage more closely with God's plan, even if it's not perfect?

_____
_____
_____

Prayer:

Take a moment to pray, asking God for wisdom in understanding His purpose for your marriage and asking for the strength to live out love, honor, and commitment.

Chapter 2
Our Idea of Marriage vs. God's Idea of Marriage

In the early years of my marriage, I focused on pleasing others and trying to meet my husband's needs based on my own expectations. When those expectations weren't met, I became frustrated, disappointed, and resentful. I even considered leaving, convinced this wasn't the life I had envisioned.

But in my lowest moment, God revealed a hard truth: I had been looking to my husband for fulfillment—something only God could provide. My dependence on him had replaced my dependence on God. The desire I had for my husband, as mentioned in Genesis 3:16, wasn't a blessing—it was misplaced worship rooted in brokenness.

Through that encounter, God reminded me that He knew me before I was ever married, and only He could truly satisfy my heart. I began seeking God first, asking Him to show me who I was as a wife and how to love my husband through His love, not my own strength.

True transformation in our marriage happens when we stop expecting our spouse to be our source and allow God to be first in our lives and marriage.

Reflection Questions:

Have you ever placed expectations on your spouse that they couldn't meet? How did that affect your relationship?

_____
_____
_____

What does it mean to you to rely on God for fulfillment instead of your spouse?

_____
_____
_____

Reflect on a time when you sought God's guidance in your marriage. How did it impact the situation or your feelings?

_____
_____
_____

In what ways can you grow closer to God in your marriage?

_____
_____
_____

Journaling Prompt:

Write about a time when you tried to change or fix your spouse, rather than focusing on your own relationship with God. How did you feel afterward? What did you learn?

_____
_____
_____

Activity: God's Design for Marriage

Step 1: Write down the qualities of God that you admire and seek to embody in your relationship (e.g., unconditional love, patience, grace).

Step 2: Discuss with your spouse how these qualities can be reflected in your marriage.

Prayer:

Pray for a heart that seeks fulfillment in God alone and for the wisdom to grow in love and honor toward your spouse.

Chapter 3
Renewing Our Commitment to God Renews Our Marriage

Marriage isn't sustained by romantic love alone—it's strengthened by our covenant with God. When I stopped trying to "fix" things and started surrendering to God, everything changed. Through prayer, humility, and a renewed mind, I began to see my husband the way God does. My love deepened—not out of need, but with the affection of Christ. If you're struggling, start with surrender. God transforms hearts, homes, and marriages—one thought, one prayer, one act of obedience at a time.

Key Scriptures:

- Philippians 1:8 – Love rooted in Christ
- James 1:19 – Wisdom for communication
- Romans 8:26–27 – Spirit-led intercession
- Romans 12:2 – Mind renewal

Reflection Questions:

1. What expectations have you placed on your spouse that may reflect control instead of surrender?
2. How have you seen God's role in your marriage? In what ways has He been a source of strength and guidance?
3. What are the areas in your marriage where you need to "renew" your commitment to God?

4. Think about a time when you saw your spouse through God's eyes. How did that change the way you interacted with them?

Activity: Renew Your Commitment

- **Step 1:** Take a moment to reflect on your relationship with God. How is your personal relationship with Him affecting your marriage?

- **Step 2:** Write a commitment statement, pledging to renew your relationship with God and your spouse. (e.g., "I commit to prioritizing my relationship with God first and my marriage second, trusting that this will strengthen both.")

Prayer:

Pray for renewal in your commitment to God and your spouse. Ask God for the strength to remain faithful to His will for your marriage.

Bonus Exercises:

Marriage Growth Plan

- Identify **three goals** you would like to work on in your marriage (communication, trust, intimacy, etc.).

- For each goal, write down **two practical steps** you can take to make progress.

- Track your progress monthly and pray for God's guidance in these areas.

Scripture Meditation:

Each week, pick a Bible verse related to marriage and meditate on it. Write it down and reflect on how you can apply it in your daily life. Some verses to consider:

- Ephesians 5:33

- 1 Corinthians 13:4-7

- Genesis 2:24

- Colossians 3:19

Chapter 4
Committing Through the Struggles

Introduction: Marriage is full of moments when life tests our commitment. Challenges like separation, financial strain, parenting difficulties, or even differing personalities can make the road feel rocky. Yet, it's in these moments of struggle that commitment becomes most significant. This chapter helps us to look beyond our immediate feelings, focus on our covenant with God and our spouse, and renew our commitment even when the journey is tough.

Reflection Questions:

1. **Commitment in Tough Times:**

   o Reflect on a difficult period in your marriage. What were the struggles you faced, and how did your commitment help you through them?

   _____
   _____
   _____

   o What does it mean for you to serve your spouse, especially in difficult times?

   _____
   _____
   _____

2. **Marriage as a Covenant:**

   o How do you understand the concept of marriage as a covenant, not just a contract?

- When you made your vows, did you fully realize the depth of commitment they involved? Reflect on how that commitment has been tested.

3. **Struggles and Perspective:**

    - Have there been times when you saw your spouse as the "enemy" in the conflict, rather than the problem itself? How did this change your approach to resolving the issue?

    - Galatians 5:16 says, "Walk by the Spirit, and you will not carry out the desires of the flesh." How can you apply this verse to your marriage when emotions run high?

4. **Trust and Faith in God's Plan:**

    - Reflect on a time when you doubted God's plan for your marriage due to your circumstances. How did you overcome that doubt? How can you strengthen your faith moving forward?

Activity: Fighting for Each Other, Not the Problem

1. **Step 1:** Think of a current or past conflict in your marriage. Instead of blaming your spouse, write down the specific problem that caused tension (e.g., finances, communication issues, family dynamics).

2. **Step 2:** Ask yourself: How can I address this problem without making my spouse feel like the enemy? What actions can I take to support my spouse in solving this issue together?

3. **Step 3:** Discuss this exercise with your spouse, acknowledging the problem and agreeing on how to face it as a team, rather than opponents.

Journaling Prompt:

- Write a letter to your spouse, not about what they've done wrong, but about how you are committed to them despite the struggles you've faced. Reflect on how you can support them through future challenges and how you plan to focus on unity.

Prayer:

Take a moment to pray, asking for God's strength to honor your marriage covenant. Ask Him to help you walk by the Spirit, especially when emotions run high, and to guide you both through any struggles that may come your way.

Chapter 5
Built for Connection, Bound by Conviction

"God built us for relationships—but not every relationship is meant to stay the same."

In this chapter, I share a deeply personal story of navigating emotional betrayal in my marriage. When emotional boundaries were crossed—not through physical infidelity, but through inappropriate emotional attachments—I found myself hurt, angry, and unheard.

I tried to confront the issue, but nothing changed. Then, during a moment of quiet prayer, I heard the gentle voice of the Holy Spirit say:

"Stop fighting a battle that isn't yours. Pray, and leave it to Me."

That whisper changed everything.

I stopped fighting with my husband and started fighting *for* him—on my knees. I surrendered the outcome to God and invited Him into the broken places of our relationship. Slowly, change began to unfold. Emotional boundaries were rebuilt. Communication was restored. And out of our healing, a deeper ministry was born.

But let me be clear: **perseverance is not the same as enduring harm**. God does not call us to stay silent in the face of emotional manipulation or disrespect. With God's guidance, prayer, and clear boundaries, healing *is* possible—even in the mess.

Reflective Questions:

1. **Where in your relationships have emotional boundaries been unclear or crossed?**
   What feelings has that stirred in you—hurt, confusion, anger, fear?

   _____
   _____

2. **Are you trying to fight a battle in your own strength that God is asking you to surrender?**
   What would it look like to release control and trust Him with the outcome?

   _____
   _____

3. **What patterns—whether from your family, past relationships, or culture—might be shaping how you approach conflict or intimacy?**
   Are there any generational cycles that need to be broken?

   _____
   _____

4. **How do you personally define emotional faithfulness in marriage or close relationships?**
   Have you and your spouse or significant others talked openly about those expectations?

   _____
   _____

5. **Is God inviting you to set new boundaries, or reinforce old ones, in love—not fear or control?**

What support (counsel, community, prayer) do you need to do that well?

_____
_____

6. **If you're in a difficult relationship season right now, what would it mean to "go to war on your knees"?**
   What might shift if you prayed first, and spoke second?

_____
_____

Prayer Prompt: Surrender and Trust

Take a moment to pray this aloud or write your own prayer below.

Lord, I release the things I've been trying to control.

I confess where I've strived, argued, or feared.

I trust You to work in the hearts I cannot change and in the places I cannot fix.

Break the cycles that have followed my family and bring healing where there has been emotional pain.

Thank you for being faithful even when I feel forgotten.

I surrender this relationship to You. Transform it—and transform me.

In Jesus' name, Amen.

Chapter 6
Restoring Your Marriage: Let Go of the Past and Choose Love

Many couples believe starting over with someone new will fix their brokenness, but unresolved guilt and unhealthy patterns follow us until we choose to confront them. True healing in marriage begins with humility, repentance, and a renewed commitment to love as Christ loves us.

Key Points:

- **Let Go of Justifications:**
  Saying "this is just who I am" or "God made me this way" can be a shield for pride. As believers, we are called to reflect Christ—not our flesh.

- **Renew Your Mind Daily:**
  A healthy marriage requires spiritual renewal through prayer, Scripture, and intentional behavior. Speak to your spouse with the same respect you'd give to God or a respected leader.

- **Broken Trust Needs Time:**
  When vows are broken, healing takes time. Forgiveness cannot be forced. Your spouse needs space, and trust must be rebuilt through consistent, changed actions—not empty promises.

- **Marriage Is a Covenant:**
  On your wedding day, you vowed to love and honor your spouse before God. Breaking that covenant impacts not just your relationship, but your spiritual walk and family.

- **True Repentance Brings Freedom:**
  Like Christ's love shown on the cross, real love requires sacrifice

and humility. Repentance breaks shame and sets your marriage free.

- **Seek Help—Don't Walk Alone:**
  Restoration often requires outside help—counselors, pastors, or mentors. Unity comes when both spouses seek healing together.

- **Choose Love Daily:**
  Let go of yesterday's disappointments. Ask yourself:
  How am I showing love to my spouse today?
  Real love is a daily choice.

Reflection Questions:

1. **Trusting God for Restoration:**

   o Think about areas in your marriage that need restoration. How can you trust God more fully with these areas?

   _____
   _____
   _____

   o How does the promise in Jeremiah 29:11 speak to your situation? Reflect on how this verse reassures you of God's plan for your marriage.

   _____
   _____
   _____

2. **Letting Go of the Past:**

   o Are there past disappointments or offenses that you are still holding onto? How can letting go of these past hurts lead to a healthier, more restored marriage?

- How do you view forgiveness? Are there areas where forgiveness is needed, either from you or your spouse?

3. **Words Matter:**

- In your marriage, how often do you speak with love and positivity, especially during difficult times? How can you be more intentional with your words to build up your spouse?

4. **Commitment to Change:**

- Do you believe that true change is possible in your marriage? How can you ensure that you are actively working to make that change happen with the help of God's grace?

5. **Forgiveness and Healing:**

- Are you holding onto guilt or shame from past mistakes in your marriage? How can you release that burden and allow God's forgiveness to heal your relationship?

- What areas in your marriage still need forgiveness? What steps are you willing to take to initiate healing?

　

6. **Choosing Love:**

- Is there a pattern or behavior you have been holding onto that is damaging your marriage? How can you break that cycle and choose love instead?

　

- How does 1 John 3:18 inspire you to turn your love for your spouse into actions rather than just feelings?

　

7. **Breaking Old Patterns:**

- Reflect on your actions and patterns that have been repeated in your marriage. Are there any habits you need to let go of in order to fully commit to your spouse and God's plan for your marriage?

Activity: Choosing to Love Every Day

Step 1: Write a list of the things you appreciate about your spouse. Be specific. How have they shown love or commitment recently?

_____
_____

Step 2: Choose one of these qualities or actions that you could mirror today. Write down how you can show love or appreciation toward them in a similar way.

_____
_____
_____

Step 3: Make a commitment to do this once a day for the next week, no matter the circumstances. Keep track of how this impacts your relationship.

☐ What behaviors or attitudes have I justified in my marriage that God may be calling me to change?

_____
_____

☐ How can I be more intentional about renewing my mind and actions each day?

_____
_____

☐ In what ways have I hurt my spouse, and what steps can I take to rebuild trust?

☐ Have I given my spouse the grace and time they need to heal? Am I being patient?

☐ How have I shown love to my spouse this week? How can I do better tomorrow?

Activity: Rebuilding Trust

Step 1: Sit down with your spouse and openly discuss areas where trust has been broken, whether recently or in the past. Be honest but kind in addressing how these events affected the relationship.

Step 2: Develop a mutual understanding of what rebuilding trust will look like for both of you. What promises can you make to each other to restore that trust?

Step 3: Pray together, asking God to help you rebuild trust and renew your hearts towards one another.

Journaling Prompt:

Love is more than a feeling—it's a decision we make every day. Feelings may come and go, but love shown through intentional, selfless action builds a lasting connection.

Reflect and Write:

What is one specific, meaningful action you will take today to show your spouse that you are committed to them and to your marriage?

_____
_____
_____

This could be a kind gesture, a word of encouragement, an act of service, or simply taking time to listen without distraction.

✍ *Write your thoughts below:*

_____

Today, I will show my spouse love by...

_____
_____
_____
_____

Prompt 2: A Letter of Repentance and Restoration

(For situations where trust has been broken or hurt has occurred)

True healing begins when we acknowledge the pain we've caused and take responsibility. Humility breaks the power of shame and pride—both for the one who was hurt and the one who caused the hurt.

Write a heartfelt letter or record a voice message to your spouse. In it:

- Acknowledge the specific pain your actions caused.

- Offer a sincere apology without making excuses.

- Express your desire and commitment to rebuild trust.
- Speak with eye contact, vulnerability, and humility.
- If possible, have a trusted witness present to bring accountability and healing.

Begin your letter here:

Dear [Spouse's Name],

I am committed to...

With God's help, I will...

Love,
[Your Name]

Healing takes courage, truth, and grace. Ask God to guide your words, soften your heart, and restore what has been broken. Speak this with love, and let Him do the rest.

Prayer:

Pray for the strength to let go of past hurts and disappointments. Ask God for the courage to actively love your spouse and work toward the restoration of your marriage, trusting Him to guide you.

Chapter 7
Staying in Love

Love isn't just a feeling—it's a daily choice. Emotions may fade, but real love is sustained through intentional actions, spiritual connection, and consistent care.

To stay in love with your spouse, you must:

- **Choose love daily**, even when it's difficult.

- **Stay emotionally connected**, especially during busy or distant seasons.

- **Show appreciation** and interest in your spouse's passions.

- **Make time to date each other**, away from kids and responsibilities.

- **Pray together** to invite God into your marriage.

- **Laugh, dance, and enjoy each other's company**—even in ordinary moments.

- **Protect your bond** from outside influences and unnecessary comparisons.

When small things start to feel big, it often signals deeper emotional or spiritual needs. Don't just treat the symptoms—step back, pray, and come together with humility. Healing and reconnection often begin with simple steps: honest conversation, shared prayer, and quiet moments of togetherness.

Key Reminder:
Your marriage is your most important assignment. Invest in it with love, time, and faith—and it will grow stronger with every season.

Reflection Questions:

1. **Daily Love Decisions:**

   o How do you intentionally show love to your spouse every day?

   _____
   _____

   o Think of one action you can do today that shows love in a new way.

2. **Connection Across Distance:**

   o How do you stay emotionally connected with your spouse when you're physically apart (work, travel, etc.)?

   _____
   _____

   o List a few ways you can improve this connection.

   _____
   _____

3. **Small Gestures of Care:**

   o What small actions or gestures have you done recently to show your spouse you care?

   _____
   _____

   o How do you think these gestures impact your marriage?

   _____
   _____

4. **Appreciation Practice:**

   - Take a moment to express your gratitude for your spouse. What are the top five things you appreciate about them?

5. **Learning Your Spouse's Passions:**

   - What are some of your spouse's hobbies or interests that you haven't paid much attention to?

   - Make a goal to show interest in at least one of these in the next week.

6. **Maintaining a Loving Connection:**

   - Have you been setting aside quality time for dates? If not, why do you think it's difficult to prioritize?

   - Plan a date or special time for the two of you this week. Write it down here.

7. **Praying Together:**

   o When was the last time you prayed with your spouse? How did it affect your relationship?

   o Set a goal to pray together at least once this week and share how it feels afterward.

8. **Facing Challenges Together:**

   o Are you finding it easy to face challenges as a team? If not, why do you think this is?

   o Discuss a current issue and plan together how to face it united.

Bible Verses for Staying in Love

1. **1 Corinthians 13:4–7 (NIV)**

   "Love is patient, love is kind. It does not envy, it does not boast, it is not proud. It does not dishonor others, it is not self-seeking, it is not easily angered, it keeps no record of wrongs. Love does not delight in evil but rejoices with the truth. It always protects, always trusts, always hopes, always perseveres."
   This verse defines love as action and commitment—not just emotion.

2. **Romans 12:10 (NIV)**

   "Be devoted to one another in love. Honor one another above yourselves."
   Lasting love begins with mutual devotion and humility.

3. **Ecclesiastes 4:9–10 (NIV)**

   "Two are better than one, because they have a good return for their labor: If either of them falls down, one can help the other up."
   Marriage is a partnership—lifting each other up through all seasons.

4. **Ephesians 4:2–3 (NIV)**

   "Be completely humble and gentle; be patient, bearing with one another in love. Make every effort to keep the unity of the Spirit through the bond of peace."
   Staying in love requires patience, gentleness, and effort to maintain unity.

5. **Song of Songs 8:7 (NIV)**

   "Many waters cannot quench love; rivers cannot sweep it away."
   True love, nurtured by God, endures through all trials.

Prayer:
Lord, thank You for the gift of marriage. Teach us to slow down, to prioritize what matters, and to love each other with patience and grace. Help us find joy in the simple moments and strength in the small acts of connection. Draw us closer to You and to each other, one day at a time. Amen.

Chapter 8
Building a Strong, Firm Foundation in Your Marriage

Marriage is a lifelong journey that requires an act of love—it demands intention, spiritual grounding, and mutual effort. As life shifts through seasons, it's easy to let distance grow and connection fade. But even in hard times, you can build a marriage that's not only lasting but thriving—one grounded in faith, friendship, and resilience.

In a fast-paced world, couples must fight against disconnection by choosing to invest in one another daily. This includes creating new memories, staying emotionally and spiritually vulnerable, and refusing to let temptation or discouragement divide you.

Naked and Not Ashamed: Restoring Honesty and Intimacy in Marriage

As believers, we are called to cultivate a marriage where **honesty**, **transparency**, and **acceptance** are the norm. As 1 John 3:18 reminds us:

"Let us not love with words or speech but with actions and in truth."

But ever since sin entered the world (Genesis 3:6–7), humanity has struggled to maintain that kind of vulnerable connection. Adam and Eve's first response after disobeying God was **shame, hiding, and blame**. They covered themselves and hid from God—and in doing so, their relationship with each other and with their Creator was fractured. Pride had crept into their hearts, and the intimacy they once knew was lost.

The same pattern can quietly play out in marriage today.

When we stop guarding our hearts and stop tending to our relationship with intention, small compromises begin to erode the foundation. **Selfishness, emotional distance, secrecy, and unchecked habits** can start to build invisible walls between us and our spouse.

Over time, we may lose our sense of conviction about things that once grieved us. We start to **normalize attitudes and behaviors** that dishonor our spouse and the covenant we made before God.

The beautiful image of being **"naked and not ashamed"** (Genesis 2:25) gets reversed. Instead of walking in emotional and spiritual openness, we begin covering ourselves in **defensiveness, pride, lust, or resentment**. We become guarded, distant, and—perhaps most tragically—we **lose the urgency to repent or restore intimacy**.

But God still calls us back. Back to the truth. Back to each other. Back to vulnerability rooted in covenant love.

Key principles for building a strong foundation:

Prioritize connection—don't let life pull you apart without resisting.

Choose unity over pride—healing often begins with a sincere apology.

Pray together and stay rooted in God's Word.

Make your home "divorce-proof" by setting spiritual boundaries and protecting your relationship from outside influences.

Cultivate emotional and physical intimacy—passion is built, not stumbled upon.

Stay open and vulnerable with each other, just as Adam and Eve were "naked and unashamed" (Genesis 2:25).

Fight for closeness through small, consistent acts of affection, kindness, and attention.

Protect your marriage like a sacred garden—tend to it with care, or weeds will take root.

Marriage isn't about being right; it's about being united.
When nurtured with prayer, transparency, grace, and effort, your

marriage becomes a secure, joy-filled place of strength for you and your family.

Reflection Questions:

1. **Handling Tough Times:**

   o   How do you stay focused on your marriage during challenging seasons?

   _____
   _____

   o   Write down one thing you can do to maintain your connection through difficult times.

   _____
   _____

2. **Compromise and Unity:**

   o   Reflect on a recent situation where you had to compromise for the sake of your marriage. How did that help?

   _____
   _____

   o   What are some compromises you may need to make in the near future?

   _____
   _____

3. **Intentional Time for Each Other:**

   o   Have you and your spouse been making intentional time for each other, despite your busy schedules?

- Brainstorm three activities you can do together that don't require much time but will strengthen your bond.

4. **Creating New Memories:**

    - Reflect on the happiest memory you share with your spouse. What made that moment special?

    - How can you create new memories together moving forward?

5. **Your "Divorce-Proof" Home:**

    - What are some practices or boundaries you can establish to protect your marriage from external influences?

    - Discuss these ideas with your spouse.

6. **Vulnerability and Openness:**

   o In what ways are you being emotionally and spiritually vulnerable with your spouse?

   _____
   _____
   _____

   o How can you improve your openness and honesty in the relationship?

   _____
   _____
   _____

7. **Resolving Conflict:**

   o Think of a recent argument or disagreement. How could you have handled it differently to maintain peace?

   _____
   _____
   _____

   o Set a goal to try resolving any future conflicts with more patience and empathy.

8. **Building Intimacy:**

   o How do you nurture both physical and emotional intimacy in your marriage?

   _____
   _____
   _____

- Create a plan to keep your connection strong, through both small acts of love and more intimate moments.

1. Reflect on your own marriage: In what ways do you feel emotionally "naked and not ashamed" with your spouse? Where might you still be holding back or covering yourself?

2. Can you identify any patterns of shame, hiding, or blame that have affected your relationship—either from past hurts or current struggles? How have these impacted your intimacy?

3. How do pride, defensiveness, or resentment show up in your marriage? What small compromises or unchecked habits might be creating emotional walls between you and your spouse?

4. Are there attitudes or behaviors you've normalized that dishonor your spouse or the sacred covenant you made before God? How can you bring these to light and invite God's healing?

5. What does it mean to you personally to love "with actions and in truth" (1 John 3:18) in your marriage? How can you practice this daily?

6. How can you invite God to help you repent and restore emotional and spiritual intimacy with your spouse?

A strong marriage is built with wisdom, intention, and care.

Bible Verses:

1. Genesis 2:25 (NIV)

2. *"Adam and his wife were both naked, and they felt no shame."*
   This verse represents emotional and spiritual vulnerability—God's original design for marriage was openness without fear or shame.

3. 1 Corinthians 13:4–5 (NIV)

4. *"Love is patient, love is kind. It does not envy, it does not boast, it is not proud. It does not dishonor others, it is not self-seeking, it is not easily angered, it keeps no record of wrongs."*
   A reminder that love in marriage must be intentional, humble, and gracious—especially during difficult seasons.

5. Philippians 1:8 (NIV)

6. *"God can testify how I long for all of you with the affection of Christ Jesus."*
Let this be a model for how deeply we are called to long for and love our spouse—with Christlike affection.

7. Ecclesiastes 4:12 (NLT)

8. *"A person standing alone can be attacked and defeated, but two can stand back-to-back and conquer. Three are even better, for a triple-braided cord is not easily broken."*
A Christ-centered marriage creates unbreakable unity and strength.

9. 1 John 3:18 (NIV)

10. *"Dear children, let us not love with words or speech but with actions and in truth."*
Love must be shown through consistent actions and authenticity—not just spoken.

11. Proverbs 24:3–4 (NLT)

12. *"A house is built by wisdom and becomes strong through good sense. Through knowledge its rooms are filled with all sorts of precious riches and valuables."*

Prayer:

Heavenly Father, thank You for the gift of marriage. In every season—through joy and hardship—help us stay grounded in Your love and truth. Teach us to be quick to forgive, patient in conflict, and intentional in our connection. Strengthen our bond, not just emotionally and physically, but spiritually. Let our home be filled with peace, our hearts open with vulnerability, and our relationship protected by Your Word. We invite you to be the foundation of our marriage. Unite us, Lord, and fill our love with purpose and passion, so that we may glorify You through our commitment to each other. In Jesus' name, Amen.

Chapter 9
Avoiding an Empty Marriage

An empty marriage doesn't always look broken on the outside—it often looks busy, productive, and functional. But beneath the surface, many couples feel emotionally disconnected. They give their time to everything except each other, and the love that once brought them together is quietly starved.

God designed marriage to be a source of deep connection and intimacy, but that fullness begins with Him. No spouse can meet the need only God was meant to fill. When we neglect our relationship with God, we often turn to our spouse, work, or distractions to feel whole—and still end up empty.

To avoid an empty marriage:

- Seek God's presence daily.

- Surrender your heart, not just your behavior.

- Love your spouse through intentional, daily actions.

- Give your best to your spouse—not what's left.

- Stay emotionally and spiritually connected.

A full marriage flows from a full heart—one rooted first in God.

Reflection Questions:

1. **Feeling Empty in Marriage:**

    o Have you ever felt disconnected or empty in your marriage? What caused these feelings?

- Write about how you can shift from emptiness to fulfillment in your relationship.

2. **Prioritizing God's Love:**

- How do you prioritize your relationship with God in your marriage?

- Take a moment to pray, asking God to fill both you and your spouse with His love and peace.

3. **Action-Based Love:**

- Are you showing love through actions, not just words? Give examples from the past week.

- Think of one new action you can take today to demonstrate love to your spouse.

4. **Overcoming Distractions:**

   - In what ways do you let work, social media, or other distractions interfere with your marriage?

   - What steps can you take to avoid these distractions and focus on your spouse?

5. **Seeking Fulfillment in God:**

   - Reflect on a time when you felt incomplete or unfulfilled. How did you turn to God for fulfillment?

   - Consider ways you and your spouse can both seek God more fully and find fulfillment in Him.

6. **Building True Connection:**

   - What are the ways you and your spouse can ensure that you stay truly connected, spiritually, emotionally, and physically?

- Write down some intentional actions you can take to create and sustain that connection.

7. **Seeking Guidance:**

    - Is there a challenge you are currently facing that requires guidance from God or wise counsel?

    - Commit to seeking help or advice from someone trustworthy and godly, if needed.

8. **Forgiveness and Healing:**

    - Have there been wounds in your marriage that need healing? What steps can you take to forgive and move forward together?

    - Write a prayer for healing and restoration for both you and your spouse.

Application Activities:

1. **Prayer Time:** Set aside time each day this week to pray for your marriage and your spouse. Keep a journal of your prayers and any answers you receive.

2. **Date Night Challenge:** Plan at least two special date nights this month. Think creatively and try to spend meaningful time with each other.

3. **Communication Exercise:** Set a goal to practice active listening with your spouse, where one person speaks, and the other listens without interrupting or offering solutions. Take turns.

4. **Forgiveness Action:** Identify any past hurts that still need healing. Discuss them with your spouse and commit to letting go of resentment and moving forward in forgiveness.

As you work through this workbook, remember that marriage is a journey, and the goal isn't perfection but growth. Let each exercise and prayer bring you closer to God and to each other. A successful marriage is built on love, grace, and commitment—both to your spouse and to God.

This workbook provides a structured approach for couples to reflect, learn, and grow in their marriage while keeping God at the center. It allows individuals to focus on self-reflection, communication, and intentional action, and incorporates prayer as a powerful tool for transformation.

Questionnaire:

Personal Information

1. **Name(s):**

   _____

2. **Date of Marriage:**

   _____

3. **How long have you been married?**

   _____

Communication

4. How would you rate the communication in your marriage (1 = poor, 10 = excellent)?
   Rating: _____
   Why?

5. What are some challenges you face in communicating with your spouse?

Conflict Resolution

6. How do you typically resolve conflicts with your spouse?

7. What would you like to improve about how you handle conflict in a Christ-centered way?

Emotional Intimacy

8. How emotionally connected do you feel with your spouse (1–10)?
   Rating: _____
   Why?

9. What can you do to strengthen emotional intimacy, keeping Christ at the center?

Shared Values and Goals

10. Do you and your spouse share similar long-term goals (faith, family, service)?

11. How do you ensure you are both aligned on spiritual and life goals?

Family and Church Life

12. How do you balance time between church, family, work, and your relationship?

13. Are there any family-related issues (e.g., in-laws, children) affecting your marriage or faith journey?

Spiritual Life

14. How important is faith and spiritual growth in your marriage?

15. How do you incorporate prayer, Bible study, or church activities into your relationship?

Personal Growth

16. How do you support each other's personal growth in Christ?

17. What spiritual growth goals do you have individually and as a couple?

Fun & Romance

18. How often do you engage in fun or romantic activities together? How do you ensure these times honor God?

19. What are some ways to add more fun and romance into your marriage, while honoring Christ?

Future Vision

20. Where do you see your marriage in 5 years—spiritually and in service to others?

21. What steps can you take to ensure your marriage thrives with Christ at the center?

Roles & Expectations

22. Are your marriage roles (chores, finances, leadership) clear and balanced? Why or why not?

23. What are some unspoken expectations you have for your spouse? Have you discussed them openly?

24. How do you navigate differences in values or interests?

Expectations from this Class

25. What do you hope to gain or learn from this class, especially regarding spiritual growth together?

Additional Reflections

26. What are some of the strengths you admire in your spouse—especially spiritually?

27. How can you work together to strengthen your relationship with God and with each other?

Vision for Marriage and Family

28. What is your vision for your marriage and family—now and in the future—in terms of faith, values, and growth?

End of Questionnaire

www.ingramcontent.com/pod-product-compliance
Lightning Source LLC
Chambersburg PA
CBHW051607010526
44119CB00056B/809